سوران جان

« تولدت مبارک »

از طرف : آیدین

Collector's Guide

Bath · New York · Cologne · Melbourne · Delhi
Hong Kong · Shenzhen · Singapore

This edition published by Parragon Books Ltd in 2016

Parragon Books Ltd
Chartist House
15–17 Trim Street
Bath BA1 1HA, UK
www.parragon.com

ISBN 978-1-4748-3630-2

Printed in China

Contents

Welcome to the totally awesome world of Disney Tsum Tsum!

This guidebook will tell you everything you need to know about all your favourite sweet and stackable friends.

Do you know where Piglet lives and what Cinderella dreams of? Can you name Bambi's BFF and do you know about Go Go's superpower?

Turn the pages to find out all the essential facts about the Disney Tsum Tusm gang - and so much more!

Mickey and Friends

Mickey

Also known as: the mouse who started it all

Personality: charming and friendly

Special ability: a powerful imagination

BFFs: Donald Duck and Pluto

Quote: "Oh, boy!"

Minnie

Personality: affectionate and free-spirited

Fashion style: bow-tastic

Likes: polka dots and making new friends

Best feature: she always sees the good in others

Quote: "Yoo-hoo!"

5

Donald

Personality: angry, opinionated and funny

Loves: his nephews Huey, Dewey and Louie

He's always: getting overexcited

Special ability: his creativity

Quote: "Aw, phooey!"

Daisy

Personality: smart, fashionable and impatient

BFF: Minnie

Loves: the colour pink, flowers and shopping

Quote: "Oh, goody!"

Pluto

Personality: playful, curious and loyal

Also known as: Pluto Pup

Dislikes: baths

Acts as: Mickey's trusty sidekick

Quote: "Yeah, yeah, yeah."

Goofy

Personality: silly, sweet and fun-loving

Full name: Goofy Goof

BFF: Mickey

Brilliant at: sports

Quote: "Aw, shucks!"

Chip 'N' Dale

Chip

Personality: logical and intelligent

How to tell him apart from Dale: he has a small black nose and a dark coat

Known as: the brains of the duo

BFF: Dale

Talent: he's super-speedy

Dislikes: trees being cut down

Quote:

"Jiminy's journal!"

Dale

Personality: carefree, loveable and adventurous

How to tell him apart from Chip: he has a red nose and a lighter coat

BFF: Chip

Favourite food: nuts

Hobby: playing tricks

Strength: his powerful teeth

Quote:

"Nuts? Where?"

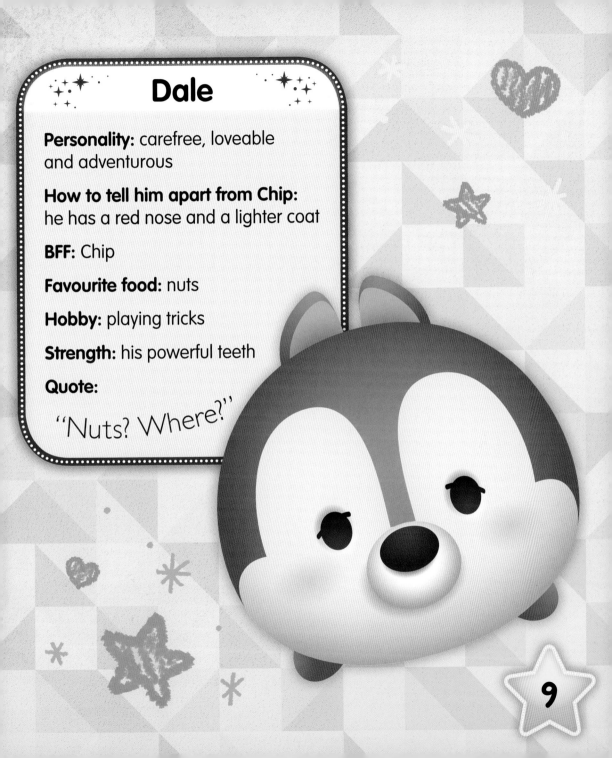

9

101 Dalmatians

Patch

Personality: fearless and adventurous

Longs to: stand out from his brothers and sisters

Role model: Pongo, his father

Favourite hobby: watching TV

Dreams of: being like Thunderbolt, his TV hero

Enemy: Cruella de Vil

Cruella de Vil

Personality: sophisticated and ambitious

Likes: money, fashion and furs

Hobby: driving her car recklessly

Dreams of: turning the 101 dalmatians into a fur coat

Dislikes: not getting her way

Home: De Vil Mansion

Quote: "I live for furs! I worship furs!"

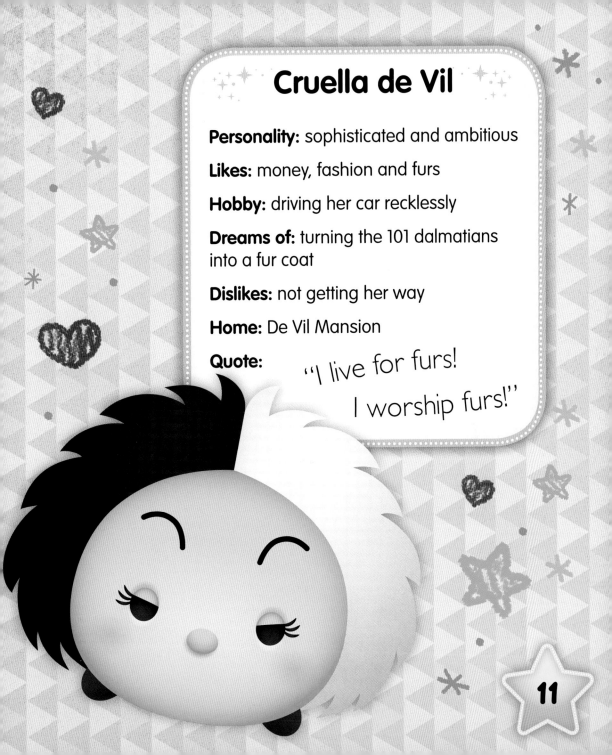

winnie the Pooh

Winnie the Pooh

Personality: loveable, caring and simple-minded

BFF: Christopher Robin

Also known as: a bear of very little brain

Happiest when: his tummy is full of honey

Greatest fear: running out of honey

Nickname: Silly Old Bear

Quote: "Oh, bother!"

12

Piglet

Personality: shy and timid

Goal: to become brave

Home: Hundred-Acre Wood

BFF: Pooh

Greatest fears: the dark, bees, danger of any kind

Favourite food: haycorns

Quote:

"Oh, d-d-d-dear! I mustn't f-f-f-fear!"

13

Tigger

Personality: energetic and boisterous

Dislikes: honey, acorns and thistles

Favourite hobbies: flying kites and bouncing

Likes: being the only tigger in the world

Best skill: his incredible bouncing abilities

Quote:

"Bouncing is what tiggers do best!"

14

Eeyore

Personality: gloomy, loyal and wise

Favourite food: prickly thistles

Likes: birthday balloons and sad stories

Enjoys: being gloomy

Best qualities: he's reliable and insightful

Favourite hobby: Pooh Sticks

Quote:

"Thanks for noticin' me."

Bambi

Bambi

Personality: curious and shy

Also known as: the Young Prince

Likes: flowers, butterflies and snow

BFF: Thumper

Dislikes: forest fires and poachers

Special skills: speed and agility

Quote:

"Mother, look! What's all that white stuff?"

Thumper

BFF: Bambi

Hobbies: thumping, hopping and having fun

Favourite food: clover blossoms

Enjoys: teaching Bambi the ways of the forest

Quote:

"I'm thumpin'! That's why they call me Thumper!"

Miss Bunny

Personality: cute and kind

BFF: Thumper

Home: the forest

Best quality: her beautiful singing voice

Quote: *"Hello!"*

17

Pinocchio

Pinocchio

Personality: happy-go-lucky, brave and friendly

Dream: to be a real boy

Hobby: dancing

Hero: his father, Geppetto

Quote: "A real boy!"

Jiminy Cricket

Personality: clever, kind and caring

Best quality: he will do anything for his friends

Good at: acting as Pinocchio's conscience

BFF: Pinocchio

Quote:  "Always let your conscience be your guide."

Figaro

Personality: curious, mischievous and easily frightened

Best feature: a heart of gold

Dislikes: baths, dogs and having to kiss Cleo

Quote:

"Meow!"

Cleo

Personality: affectionate and innocent

Favourite food: cake

Likes: kisses from Figaro

Best skills: she can twirl and jump!

19

Lady and the Tramp

Lady

Personality: romantic and sweet

BFF: Tramp

Nickname: Pidge

Favourite food: spaghetti

Dislikes: cats and muzzles

Goal: to keep her family safe

Quote:
"I should have been home hours ago."

Tramp

Personality: laid-back, fun-loving and heroic

Known as: a rogue loner … until he met Lady

BFF: Lady

Dislikes: the Dogcatcher

Biggest dream: to have a family

Special skill: he's very streetwise

Quote: "Aw, come on, kid. Start building some memories."

21

Alice in wonderland

Alice

Personality: imaginative and very curious

Loves to: daydream

Has a tendency to: get lost

Likes: books with pictures, tea parties and cats

Quote:

"Curiouser and curiouser."

White Rabbit

Personality: jittery, fidgety and highly strung

Always carries: a watch

Dislikes: being late

Fears: monsters and the Queen of Hearts

Quote: *"I'm late! I'm late for a very important date!"*

Cheshire Cat

Personality: mysterious and unpredictable

Special skills: shapeshifting and invisibility

Home: Wonderland

Enjoys: tricking people, especially Alice

Quote: *"Almost everyone's mad here."*

Curious Oyster

Personality: childish and playful

Home: Wonderland

Hobbies: sleeping and playing

Dislikes: months with 'r' in them

23

Woody

Personality: brave and loyal

Also known as: Sheriff Woody

BFF: Buzz Lightyear

Biggest fear: being replaced or forgotten

Loves: spending time with Andy

Goal: to keep the toys together

Quote: "This is a perfect time to panic!"

24

Buzz Lightyear

Personality: heroic, funny and caring

Occupation: space ranger

Also known as: Space Toy, El Buzzo

BFF: Woody

Crush: Jessie the cowgirl

Special skills: karate-chop action and he can glow in the dark

Quote: ''To infinity ... and beyond!''

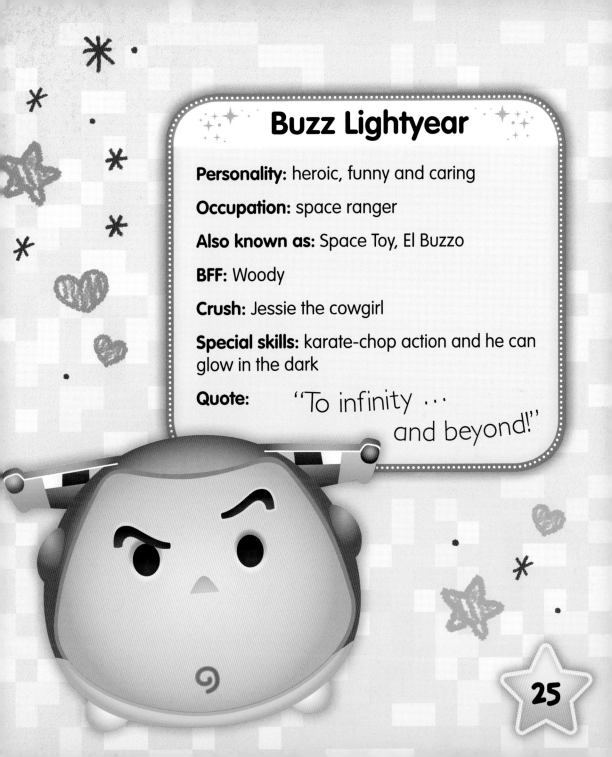

Jessie

Personality: friendly and excitable

Known as: the Yodelling Cowgirl

Greatest fear: being put into storage

BFF: Buzz Lightyear

Nickname: Princess of the Prairie

Loves: being loved

Quote: "Yee-haw!"

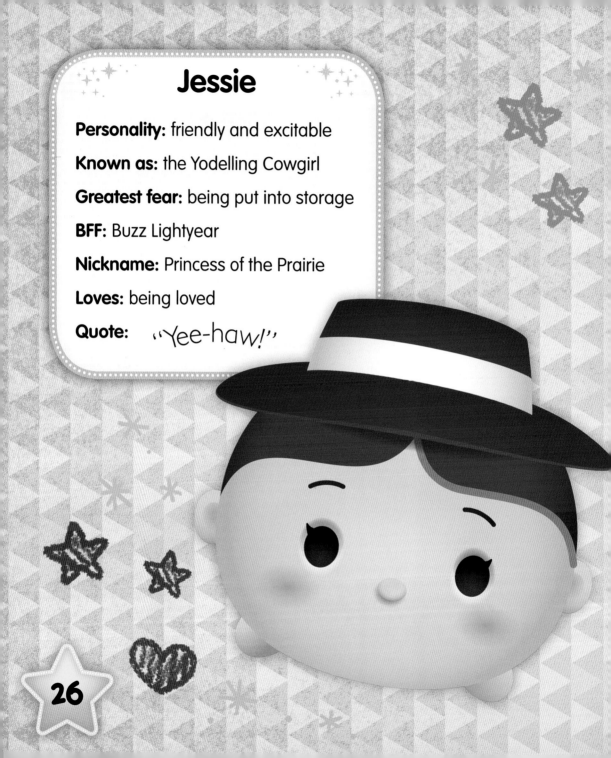

Stinky Pete

Personality: seemingly kind and wise

Also known as: The Prospector

Dislikes: space toys and children

Weapon: his pickaxe

Likes: watching Woody's Roundup on TV

Quote: *''Children destroy toys!''*

27

Bullseye

Personality: good-hearted, playful and excitable

Known as: the bravest horse in the West

Acts like: a puppy dog

BFF: Jessie the rootin' tootin' cowgirl

Dreams of: reuniting Woody's Roundup gang

Hamm

Known as: the wise-cracking, sarcastic piggy bank

Alter ego: Evil Dr Porkchop

Secret talent: he's a technological genius

Greatest fear: being abandoned

Quote:
"You heard of Kung Fu? Well, get ready for 'pork chop'!"

The Aliens

They come from: Pizza Planet

Hero: The Claw

Look up to: Mr Potato Head, their foster father

Also known as: Little Green Men, Martian Men

Quote:
"You have saved our lives. We are eternally grateful."

Three Peas in a Pod

Personality: practical, curious and loyal

Also known as: Peatey, Peatrice and Peanelope

Dislike: Lots-o'-Huggin' Bear

Hobbies: annoying Mr Potato Head

Quote: "Who's the new guy?"

29

Frozen

Elsa

Personality: elegant and caring

BFF: her sister, Anna

Greatest fear: hurting Anna

Strengths: she's a natural leader

Magical power: she can create snow and ice

Loves: using her magical powers

Quote: "Let it go!"

Anna

Personality: optimistic and loving

Hobbies: daydreaming, dancing and ice skating

Strength: her imagination

Home: Arendelle

Loves: meeting new people

BFF: her sister, Elsa

Quote: "Do you wanna build a snowman?"

31

Olaf

Personality: goofy and loveable

Loves to: daydream about summertime

Best quality: he's always happy

BFF: Sven the reindeer

Least favourite colour: yellow

Special skill: he can come apart and put himself back together again

Quote: *"Some people are worth melting for ... just not right this minute."*

Sven

Personality: loyal and brave

Occupation: ice-gatherer and sled-puller

Favourite food: carrots

Dislikes: wolves and slippery ice

Enjoys: being sung to by Kristoff

BFFs: Kristoff and Olaf

33

The Little Mermaid

Ariel

Personality: spirited, adventurous and stubborn

BFF: Flounder

Loves: humans and human objects

Talents: speed-swimming and her melodic voice

Dislikes: Ursula

Hobbies: chasing her dreams and having fun with Flounder

Quote:

"I wanna be where the people are."

34

Flounder

Personality: anxious and loyal

Best feature: he's always there for Ariel

Tends to: scare easily and panic in stressful situations

BFF: Ariel

Best swimming tricks: the 'corkscrew' and the 'torpedo tube'

Quote: "Arieeeeeeeeel!"

35

Sebastian

Personality: loyal, grumpy and funny

Occupation: Royal Court Composer

Favourite hobby: singing

Musical influences: reggae and calypso

Wishes: that he could swim faster

Comes from: Jamaica

Quote: "Under de sea!"

Scuttle

Personality: eccentric, clumsy and funny

Full name: Scuttlebutt

Hobby: collecting human objects

Dislikes: storms and predator birds

Special skills: he can swim and fly

Likes to think: he's an expert on humans

Quote: *"It's a dinglehopper!"*

King Triton

Personality: strict, serious and over-protective

Occupation: King of Atlantica

Goal: to keep the sea safe

Likes: music

Dislikes: humans

Enemy: Ursula

Quote: *"Humans are dangerous!"*

Ursula

Personality: power-hungry and sinister

Wish: to rule the seas

Likes: power

Special skills: she can make magical potions and cast spells

Pets: her beloved eels

Hobby: causing despair

Quote: *"Triton's daughter will be mine!"*

Snow white and the Seven Dwarfs

Snow White

Personality: sweet, gentle and kind

Hobbies: singing, dancing and cooking

Loves: all animals

Also known as: the fairest of them all

Quote: *"Someday my prince will come."*

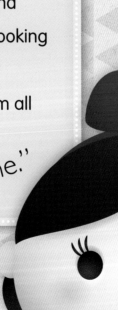

Doc

Personality: kind-hearted and bossy

Occupation: leader of the dwarfs

Dislikes: Grumpy's rude remarks

Favourite food: gooseberry pies

Quote:
"Come on, hen, uh, men. Follow me."

Grumpy

Personality: short-tempered and cheeky

Nickname: Grump-ster

Is always: losing his temper

Has a soft spot for: Snow White

Quote: "I'm warnin' ya…"

41

Bashful

Personality: shy, nervous and gentle

Has a tendency to: blush a lot

Occupation: diamond miner

Likes: Snow White, diamonds

Quote:
"Ohhh, go-o-o-osh."

Sneezy

Personality: kind and thoughtful

Dislikes: hay fever and danger

Enemy: the Evil Queen

He's always: sneezing

Quote:
"AH-CHOO-OO-OOOO!"

Sleepy

Personality: friendly and tired

Home: Cottage of the Seven Dwarfs

Dislikes: losing sleep

Likes: music, Snow White

Quote: "Zzzzzzzzzz."

Happy

Personality: optimistic and jolly

Hobbies: singing and yodelling

Loves: food, dancing and laughter

Dislikes: washing

Quote:

"Happy, ma'am. That's me."

Dopey

Personality: clumsy and playful

Known as: the baby of the group

Dislikes: talking

He's always: trying to keep up with the other dwarfs

Aladdin

Aladdin

Personality: optimistic and fun-loving

Home: Agrabah

Dreams of: seeing the world

Likes: spending time with Jasmine

Nicknames: Street Rat, Prince of Ali Ababwa

Hobbies: going on adventures and getting into trouble

Quote: "You're only in trouble if you get caught."

Jasmine

Personality: feisty and independent

Nicknames: Jaz, Princess

Best quality: she always stands up for what is right

Isn't afraid: to speak her mind

Dream: to marry for love

Dislikes: Jafar

Quote: *"If I do marry, I want it to be for love."*

Genie

Personality: flamboyant, fun-loving and hilarious

Occupation: genie of the lamp

Likes: freedom

Special abilities: his amazing cosmic powers

Best feature: he always uses his magic for good

Dislikes: living in the lamp

Quote: *"You ain't never had a friend like me!"*

46

Abu

Personality: sneaky and clever

Occupation: thief

BFF: Aladdin

Loves: shiny objects and bananas

Dislikes: danger

Known as: Aladdin's partner in crime

Quote: "Uh-oh."

47

Rajah

Personality: loyal and caring

Occupation: Jasmine's pet tiger

Goal: to protect Jasmine

Best feature: his bravery

Dislikes: Jasmine being in danger

Special skill: his amazing strength

Sultan

Personality: gullible and kind

Full name: Sultan Hamed II of Agrabah

Occupation: ruler of Agrabah

Enemy: Jafar

Hobby: riding his magic carpet

Quote: "Learn to have a little fun!"

48

Jafar

Personality: cunning and dishonest

Enjoys: scheming

Special abilities: alchemy and dark magic

Weapon: his snake staff

Quote: "There are things so much worse than death!"

49

Peter Pan

Peter Pan

Personality: fearless and heroic

Dislikes: the idea of growing up

Home: Never Land

Enemy: Captain Hook

Quote: "Second star to the right and straight on till morning!"

Wendy

Personality: motherly and caring

Hobbies: flying and dreaming

Pet: Nana the dog

Best at: telling stories

Quote: "How do we get to Never Land?"

John

Personality: brave and clever

Interests: pirates

Good at: being a leader

Loves: Wendy's stories

Quote: "Jim-a-nee!"

Michael

Personality: sensitive and playful

Favourite toy: his teddy bear

Dreams of: going on adventures

Enjoys: dancing with the Indians

Quote: "I wanna see my mother."

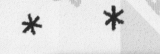

51

Tiger Lily

Personality: brave and proud

BFF: Peter Pan

Occupation: princess of the Indian tribe

Favourite hobby: dancing

Quote: "Help!"

Captain Hook

Personality: arrogant and cowardly

Also known as: the World's Most Famous Crook

Likes: treasure and power

Good at: sword fighting

Quote: "Blast that Peter Pan!"

Smee

Personality: good-natured and clumsy

Likes: treasure and pleasing Captain Hook

Dreams of: plundering the seven seas

Fears: the wrath of Captain Hook

Quote: "Cap'n!"

The crocodile

Also known as: Tick-tock Crock

Home: Crocodile Creek

He's always: hungry

Favourite food: Captain Hook

Quote: "Tick tock tick tock!"

Big Hero 6

Hiro Hamada

Hero: Tadashi, his older brother

Always tries to: look for a new angle

Interests: robots and technology

Hobby: robot fighting

Special ability: his amazing intelligence

Attends: San Fransokyo Institute of Technology

Quote: "Trust me, I know about robotics."

Baymax

Personality: clumsy, loveable and selfless

Nickname: Balloon Man

Talents: healing, rocket-powered flight

BFF: Hiro

Dislikes: pain and danger

Likes: hugs, flying and helping others

Quote: "I will always be with you."

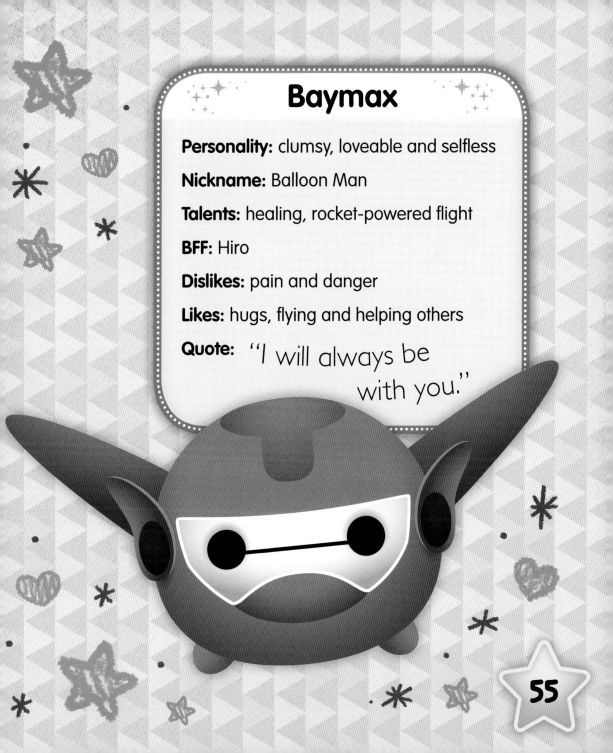

Go Go Tomago

Personality: strong, sporty and sarcastic

Special weapons: maglev discs

Super power: her amazing speed

Best quality: she'll do anything to protect her friends

Quote: "Stop whining, woman up."

Honey Lemon

Personality: eccentric, sweet and bubbly

Hobby: fashion design

Favourite colour: pink

Secret weapons: chem-balls

Quote: "That was amazing!"

56

Wasabi No-Ginger

Personality: neurotic and talented

Dislikes: heights

Weapons: plasma blades

Favourite hobby: martial arts

Quote: ''If I wasn't terrified of heights, I'd probably love this.''

Fred

Personality: creative, friendly and laid-back

Likes: comic books

Favourite hobby: playing video games

Super powers: fire breath and super bounce

Quote: ''How cool is that?!''

57

Lilo and Stitch

Lilo

Personality: sweet, polite and mischievous

Pet: Stitch

Favourite singer: Elvis Presley

Least favourite food: broccoli

Quote:

"'Ohana' means family, and family means nobody gets left behind or forgotten."

58

Stitch

Personality: childish and fun-loving

BFF: Lilo

Also known as: Experiment 626

Dislikes: water, rejection and being alone

Special abilities: superhuman strength and computer intelligence

Quote: "I'm fluffy!"

Scrump

Occupation: Lilo's doll

BFF: Lilo

Likes: hugs

Is always: having to be repaired by Lilo

Cinderella

Cinderella

Nickname: Cinderelly

BFFs: Jaq and Gus (the mice)

Loves: going to balls

Dislikes: housework

Hobbies: dancing and singing

Special ability: she can speak to animals

Dreams of: living happily ever after

Quote: "Have courage and be kind."

Sleeping Beauty

Maleficent

Pet: Diablo, her raven

Also known as: the mistress of all evil

Home: The Forbidden Mountain

Dislikes: not being invited to parties

Magical powers: teleportation and hypnosis

Hobbies: gaining revenge and causing chaos

Quote: "You poor simple fools."

61

Dumbo

Dumbo

Personality: innocent, shy and playful

Dislikes: clowns

Favourite food: peanuts

BFF: Timothy Q. Mouse

Likes: being with his mother and flying

Also known as: Jumbo, Jr

Aristocats

Marie

Personality: ladylike and feisty

Special talent: singing

Hobby: daydreaming

Looks up to: Duchess, her mother

Home: Madame Bonfamille's mansion

Likes: being the best

Quote:

"Ladies do not start fights, but they can finish them!"

63

Phineas and Ferb

Perry

Personality: silent and resourceful

Occupation: household pet

Secret occupation: secret agent

Works for: The Organization Without a Cool Acronym

Arch-nemesis: Dr Heinz Doofenshmirtz

Also known as: Agent P, P to the P